Notations:

Quotations on Music

Notations:
Quotations on Music

Edited by Sallye Leventhal

BARNES
&NOBLE
BOOKS
NEW YORK

The quotes in this book have been drawn from many sources, and are assumed to be accurate as quoted in their previously published forms. Although every effort has been made to verify the quotes and sources, the publisher cannot guarantee their perfect accuracy.

2003 Barnes & Noble Books

ISBN 0-7607-4070-4

Printed and bound in the United States of America

M 9 8 7 6 5 4 3 2 1

FROM THE FIRST LULLABIES SUNG TO US AS INFANTS, the nursery rhymes and chanting games of childhood, we begin to understand that music has a vibrant, living shape, a pulse, a voice. Each piece of music that we hear, sing, or play contributes to a sort of intuitive dialogue of musical intelligence. We learn "in our bones" the unique interplay between rhythm and dynamics, musical line, tonality and harmony. These elements within a piece speak to each other. Also, one piece of music can echo the notes and phrases of other compositions we've heard along the way; one building on and challenging another.

This journey toward musical awareness is very often not described in words. The music speaks for itself and in many ways describes its composer. Beethoven's Fifth Symphony seems to conjure in perhaps an inarticulate way what

I like to think of as aspects of Beethoven's personality; likewise the music of Duke Ellington, George Gershwin, Elvis Costello, or Frank Zappa.

Searching out these quotes on music revealed these personalities in a wholly new way. I found that my "metaphoric conversation" has a very real corollary in a chorus of distinct, opinionated, cranky, poetic, insightful voices. As I read them, one quote would bring to mind one I'd read earlier and lead seemingly inevitably to another, and another, and another. My hope is that as you read through book, or drop in here and there, that you find yourself equally caught up in the musical conversation.

—SALLYE LEVENTHAL

Notations

Music, the perfume of hearing, probably began as a religious act, to arouse groups of people. Drums set the heart sprinting in no time and a trumpet can transport one on chariots of sound. As far back as we can see, people made music.

—DIANE ACKERMAN

It is cruel, you know, that music should be so beautiful. It has the beauty of loneliness and of pain: of strength and freedom. The beauty of disappointment and never-satisfied love. The cruel beauty of nature, and everlasting beauty of monotony.

—BENJAMIN BRITTEN

When my hoe tinkled against the stones, that music echoed to the woods and the sky, and was an accompaniment to my labor which yielded an instant and immeasurable crop. It was no longer beans that I hoed, nor I that hoed beans; and I remembered with as much pity as pride, if I remembered at all, my acquaintances who had gone to the city to attend the oratorios.

—HENRY DAVID THOREAU

All art constantly aspires towards the condition of music.

—WALTER PATER

In you come with your cold music till I creep
Through every nerve.

—ROBERT BROWNING

Music rearranges your molecular structure.

—CARLOS SANTANA

Got time to breathe, got time for music.

—MR. BRISCOE DARLING, *Andy Griffith Show*

Music heard so deeply
That it is not heard at all, but you are the music
While the music lasts.

—T. S. ELIOT

Music is my mistress, and she plays second fiddle
to no one.

—DUKE ELLINGTON

This is my music; this is myself.

—RALPH WALDO EMERSON

If a man does not keep pace with his companions, perhaps it is because he hears a different drummer. Let him step to the music which he hears, however measured or far away.

—HENRY DAVID THOREAU

The great challenge which faces us is to assure that, in our society of big-ness, we do not strangle the voice of creativity, that the rules of the game do not come to overshadow its purpose, that the grand orchestration of society leaves ample room for the man who marches to the music of another drummer.

—HUBERT HUMPHREY

The man that hath no music in himself,
Nor is not mov'd with concord of sweet sounds,
Is fit for treasons, stratagems and spoils;
The motion of his spirit are dull as night
And his affections dark as Erebus:
Let no such man be trusted.

—WILLIAM SHAKESPEARE

Music was my refuge. I could crawl into the spaces between the notes and curl my back to loneliness.

—MAYA ANGELOU

Yet there is one thing the world with all its rotten-ness cannot take from us, and that is the deep and abiding joy and consolation perpetuate in great music. Here the spirit may find home and relief when all else fails.

—ERIC FENBY

When I hear music, I fear no danger. I am invulner-able. I see no foe. I am related to the earliest times, and to the latest.

—HENRY DAVID THOREAU

Wouldst thou know if a people be well governed, or if its laws be good or bad, examine the music it practices.

—CONFUCIUS

How good bad music and bad reasons sound when we are marching into battle against an enemy.

—FRIEDRICH NIETZSCHE

He who joyfully marches to music in rank and file has already earned my contempt. He has been given a large brain by mistake, since for him the spinal cord would fully suffice.

—ALBERT EINSTEIN

There is nothing stable in the world; uproar's your only music.

—JOHN KEATS

Music, to create harmony, must investigate discord.

—PLUTARCH

True music must repeat the thought and inspirations of the people and the time. My people are Americans and my time is today.

—GEORGE GERSHWIN

We are not an aria country. We are a song country.

—ALAN JAY LERNER

I know only two tunes; one of them is "Yankee Doodle", and the other isn't.

—ULYSESS S. GRANT

The truest expression of a people is in its dances and its music.

—AGNES DE MILE

I don't give a damn about "The Missouri Waltz" but I can't say it out loud because it's the song of Missouri. It's as bad as "The Star-Spangled Banner" so far as music is concerned.

—HARRY S TRUMAN

There is something suspicious about music, gentlemen. I insist that she is, by her nature, equivocal. I shall not be going too far in saying at once that she is politically suspect.

—THOMAS MANN

For the introduction of a new kind of music must be shunned as imperiling the whole state; since styles of music are never disturbed without affecting the most important political institutions.

—PLATO

If you really believe music is dangerous, you should let it go in one ear and out the other.

—JOSÉ BERGAMÍN

I wrote a song about dental floss but did anyone's teeth get cleaner?

—FRANK ZAPPA (in response to Tipper Gore's allegations that music incites people or influences their behavior in general)

Music, feelings of happiness, mythology, faces worn by time, certain twilights and certain places, want to tell us something, or they told us something that we should not have missed, or they are about to tell us something; this imminence of a revelation that is not produced is, perhaps, the esthetic event.

—JORGE LUIS BORGES

The best music always results from ecstacies of logic.

—ALBAN BERG

All good music resembles something. Good music stirs by its mysterious resemblance to the objects and feelings which motivated it.

—JEAN COCTEAU

The history of a people is found in its songs.

—GEORGE JELLINEK

Jazz came to America three hundred years ago in chains.

—PAUL WHITEMAN

The music of an unhappy people, of the children of disappointment; they tell of death and suffering and unvoiced longing toward a truer world, of misty wanderings and hidden ways.

—W. E. B. DU BOIS

It is only in his music, which Americans are able to admire because a protective sentimentality limits their understanding of it, that the Negro in America has been able to tell his story.

—JAMES BALDWIN

The white youth of today have begun to react to the fact that the "American Way of Life" is a fossil of history. What do they care if their old baldheaded and crew-cut elders don't dig their caveman mops? They couldn't care less about the old, stiff-assed honkies who don't like their new dances: Frug, Monkey, Jerk, Swim, Watusi. All they know is that it feels good to swing to way-out body-rhythms instead of drag-assing across the dance floor like zombies to the dead beat of mind-smothered Mickey Mouse music.

—ELDRIDGE CLEAVER

The new sound-sphere is global. It ripples at great speed across languages, ideologies, frontiers and races.... The economics of this musical Esperanto is staggering. Rock and pop breed concentric worlds of fashion, setting and life-style. Popular music has brought with it sociologies of private and public manner, of group solidarity. The politics of Eden come loud.

—GEORGE STEINER

Folk music is the original melody of man; it is the musical mirror of the world.

—Friedrich Nietzsche

All music is folk music. I ain't never heard no horse sing a song.

—Louis Armstrong

A nation creates music—the composer only arranges it.

—Bela Bartok

The way to write American music is simple. All you have to do is be an American and then write any kind of music you wish.

—Virgil Thomson

As the music is, so are the people of the country.

—TURKISH PROVERB

The manner in which Americans "consume" music has a lot to do with leaving it on their coffee tables, or using it as wallpaper for their lifestyles, like the score of a movie—it's consumed that way without any regard for how and why it's made.

—FRANK ZAPPA

If there is a gratification which I envy any people in this world it is to your country [Italy] its music. This is the favorite passion of my soul, and fortune has cast my lot in a country where it is in a state of deplorable barbarism.

—THOMAS JEFFERSON

This land is your land & this land is my land—
sure—but the world is run by those that never
listen to music anyway.

—Bob Dylan

Men profess to be lovers of music, but for the most
part they give no evidence of it in their opinions
and lives that they have heard it. It would not leave
them narrow-minded and bigoted.

—Henry David Thoreau

People who make music together cannot be
enemies, at least while the music lasts.

—Paul Hindemith

Have you ever been up in your plane at night, alone, somewhere, 20,000 feet above the ocean?... Did you ever hear music up there?... It's the music a man's spirit sings to his heart, when the earth's far away and there isn't any more fear. It's the high, fine, beautiful sound of an earth-bound creature who grew wings and flew up high and looked straight into the face of the future. And caught, just for an instant, the unbelievable vision of a free man in a free world.

—Dalton Trumbo and Victor Fleming.

The trumpet shall be heard on high,
The dead shall live, the living die,
And Music shall untune the sky.

—John Dryden

Music is the art which is most nigh to tears and memory.

—Oscar Wilde

I didn't sing a note the whole time I was in [prison]. I didn't feel like singing.... A lot of the girls in there...used to beg me to perform.... If they'd understand my kind of singing, they'd have known I couldn't sing in a place like that. The whole basis of my singing is feeling.... In the whole time I was there, I didn't feel a thing.

—BILLIE HOLIDAY

Music is a controlled outcry from the quarry of emotions all humans share.

—DIANE ACKERMAN

Music, when soft voices die,
Vibrates in the memory—
Odours, when sweet violets sicken,
Live within the sense they quicken.

—PERCY BYSSHE SHELLEY

For I have learned
To look on nature, not as in the hour
Of thoughtless youth, but hearing oftentimes
The still, sad music of humanity.

—WILLIAM WORDSWORTH

...she whispered a song along the keyboard to Mal
Waldron and everyone and I stopped breathing

—FRANK O'HARA

Then you've a hunch what the music meant....
hunger and night and the stars.

—ROBERT W. SERVICE

And the night shall be filled with music, and the
cares that infest the day shall fold their tents like
the Arabs, and as silently steal away.

—HENRY WADSWORTH LONGFELLOW

With music we are trapped in time. Each note is gone as soon as it has sounded and it never can be recontemplated or heard again at the particular instant of rightness. It is always too late for a second look.

—LEONARD BERNSTEIN

The whole problem can be stated quite simply by asking, 'Is there a meaning to music?' My answer to that would be, 'Yes.' And 'Can you state in so many words what the meaning is?' My answer to that would be, 'No.'

—AARON COPLAND

Music is the shorthand of emotion. Emotions, which let themselves be described in words with such difficulty, are directly conveyed to man in music, and in that is its power and significance.

—LEO TOLSTOY

Music goes deeper than emotion into the energies that animate our psychic life.

—ROGER SESSIONS

Music should go right through you, leave some of itself inside you, and take some of you with it when it leaves.

—HENRY THREADGILL

The soul of music slumbers in the shell
Till waked and kindled by the master's spell;
And feeling hearts, touch them but rightly, pour
A thousand melodies unheard before!

—SAMUEL ROGERS

Music is your own experience, your own thoughts, your wisdom. If you don't live it, it won't come out of your horn.

—CHARLIE PARKER

They'd been in the folk mass choir when they were in school but that, they knew now, hadn't really been singing. Jimmy said that real music was sex... They were starting to Agree with him. And there wasn't much sex in Morning Has Broken or The Lord Is My Shepherd.

—RODDY DOYLE

Keep it simple, keep it sexy, keep it sad.

—MITCH MILLER, on composing popular music

We all have idols. Play like anyone you care about but try to be yourself while you're doing so.

—B. B. KING

If ya ain't got it in ya, ya can't blow it out.

—LOUIS ARMSTRONG

All of one's life is music, if one touches the notes rightly, and in time.

—JOHN RUSKIN

If you hit a wrong note, then make it right by what you play afterwards.

—JOE PASS

Every actor and musician has a text upon which to base his art, but he can treat the text in one of two ways.... In music, this means asking how far the system of musical signs printed on the page can actually represent the music the composer heard in his head. If you believe these signs—the notes, the loud and soft markings, tempo indications—are an adequate language, then in performing the piece you concentrate on realizing in sound what you, the performer, read. If you believe music cannot be adequately notated, then your task in the performance is to find what is missing from the printed page.

—RICHARD SENNETT

Practice in minute detail until every note is imbued with internal life and has taken its place in the overall design.

—PABLO CASALS

Only a teacher can provide the push that allows the infinite perfectibility of music to take flight.

—THAD CARHART

When you read music, there is a part of your creativity that shuts down. It's like learning to paint with coloring books. It's like coloring within the lines—you don't take off. When you think about it, what music notes or a coloring book does is stifle creativity.

—DAVID LYNCH

I can't stand to sing the same song the same way two nights in succession, let alone two years or ten years. If you can, then it ain't music, it's close-order drill or exercise or yodeling or something, not music.

—BILLIE HOLIDAY

Improvisation is the only art form in which the same note can be played night after night but differently each time. It is the hidden things, the subconscious that lets you know you feel this, you play this.

—ORNETTE COLEMAN

I improvised, crazed by the music.... Even my teeth and eyes burned with fever. Each time I leaped I seemed to touch the sky and when I regained earth it seemed to be mine alone.

—JOSEPHINE BAKER

Music, moody food of us that trade in love.

—WILLIAM SHAKESPEARE

Through vibration comes motion;
Through motion comes color;
Through color comes tone.

—PYTHAGORAS

The exercise of singing is delightfull to Nature,
& good to preserve the health of Man.

—WILLIAM BYRD

When in doubt, sing loud.

—ROBERT MERRILL

The high note is not the only thing.

—PLACIDO DOMINGO

Am I afraid of high notes? Of course I am afraid!
What sane man is not?

—Luciano Pavarotti

Singing is a trick to get people to listen to music
for longer than they would ordinarily.

—David Byrne

Anything that is too stupid to be spoken is sung.

—Voltaire

Swans sing before they die—'twere no bad thing,
did certain persons die before they sing.

—Samuel Taylor Colderidge

People are wrong when they say opera is not what it used to be. It is what it used to be. That's what's wrong with it.

—NOEL COWARD

How wonderful opera would be if there were no singers.

—GIOACCHINO ROSSINI

No good opera plot can be sensible, for people do not sing when they are feeling sensible.

—W. H. AUDEN

Opera in English is, in the main, about as sensible as baseball in Italian.

—H. L. MENCKEN

The English do not like music but love the noise it makes.

—Sir Thomas Beecham

The French are the wittiest, the most charming, and (up to the present, at all events) the least musical race on Earth.

—Stendhal

Of all noises, I think music is the least disagreeable.

—Samuel Johnson

The moment of passage from disturbance into harmony is that of the intensest life.

—John Dewey

Alas! All music jars when the soul's out of tune.

—MIGUEL DE CERVANTES

Bad music disturbs me, but wonderful music disturbs me even more.

—ARTURO BENEDETTI MICHELANGELLI

The concert is a polite form of self-induced torture.

—HENRY MILLER

Performance is a crucifixion.

—CHARLES GOUNOD

My great sadness is the realization that the first ten minutes of every concert are lost to me, while I get accustomed all over again to being there. In these ten or fifteen minutes, I suffer agony, because even if it is a heavenly piece of music, I can't feel deeply about it, as I am still in the process of getting over my embarrassment and discomfort. When this short but oh so long time has run its miserable course, I am all right, but until then, I must submit meekly to slips of the fingers, and to a heart that beats, but not enough to obliterate me, which is what I want.... I am nervous and apprehensive because I may not "have it" that particular night. Because I feel the piece is bigger than me, so big I may never be able to even touch it, let alone be the master.

—William Kapell

More significant than the fact that poets write abstrusely, painters paint abstractly, and composers compose unintelligible music is that people should admire what they cannot understand; indeed, admire that which has no meaning or principle.

—ERIC HOFFER

Beauty in music is too often confused with something that lets the ear lie back in an easy chair. Many sounds that we are used to do not bother us, and for that reason we are inclined to call them beautiful. Frequently—possibly almost invariably—analytical and impersonal test will show that when a new or unfamiliar work is accepted as beautiful on its first hearing, its fundamental quality is one that tends to put the mind to sleep.

—CHARLES IVES

Perhaps all music, even the newest, is not so much something discovered as something that re-emerges from where it lay buried in the memory, inaudible as a melody cut in a disc of flesh. A composer lets me hear a song that has always been shut up silent within me.

—JEAN GENET

When people hear good music, it makes them homesick for something they never had and never will have.

—EDGAR WATSON HOWE

Give me a laundry list and I'll set it to music.

—GIOACCHINO ANTONIO ROSSINI

People compose for many reasons: to become immortal; because the pianoforte happens to be open; because they want to become a millionaire; because of the praise of friends; because they have looked into a pair of beautiful eyes; for no reason whatsoever.

—ROBERT SCHUMANN

My idea is that there is music in the air, music all around us, the world is full of it and you simply take as much as you require.

—SIR EDWARD ELGAR

I carry my thoughts about with me for a long time...
before writing them down...once I have grasped a
theme. I shall not forget it even years later. I change
many things, discard others, and try again and again
until I am satisfied; then, in my head...[the work]
rises, it grows, I hear and see the image in front
of me from every angle...and only the labor of
writing it down remains.... I turn my ideas into
tones that resound, roar, and rage until at last they
stand before me in the form of notes.

—Ludwig van Beethoven

Musical creativity comprises one of the mind
brain's most basic forms of intelligence—of equal
importance with linguistics, logical, mathematical
and interpersonal attitudes.

—Howard Gardner

Songwriting is about getting the demon out of me. It's like being possessed. You try to go to sleep, but the song won't let you. So you have to get up and make it into something, and then you're allowed to sleep. It's always in the middle of the bloody night, or when you're half-awake or tired, when your critical faculties are switched off. So letting go is what the whole game is. Every time you try to put your finger on it, it slips away. You turn on the lights and the cockroaches run away. You can never grasp them.

—John Lennon

The question is whether a noble song is produced by nature or by knowledge. I neither believe in mere labor being of avail without a rich vein of talent, nor in natural ability which is not educated.

—Horace

It is a wise tune that knows its own father, and I like my music to be the legitimate offspring of respectable parents.

—SAMUEL BUTLER

Bach is like an astronomer who, with the help of ciphers, finds the most wonderful stars... Beethoven embraced the universe with the power of his spirit... I do not climb so high. A long time ago I decided that my universe will be the soul and heart of man.

—FREDERIC CHOPIN

The soul of man is like the rolling world,
One half in day, the other dipt in night;
The one has music and the flying cloud,
The other, silence and the wakeful stars.

—ALEXANDER SMITH

It is the duty of the composer to serve his fellow man, to beautify human life and point the way to a radiant future. Such is the immutable code of the artist as I see it.

—SERGEI PROKOFIEV

The aim and final end of all music should be none other than the glory of God and the refreshment of the soul.

—JOHANNES SEBASTIAN BACH

Study Bach. There you will find everything.

—JOHANNES BRAHMS

Do things, act. Make a list of the music you love, then learn it by heart. And when you are writing music of your own, write it as you hear it inside and never strain to avoid the obvious.

—NADIA BOULANGER

Before I compose a piece, I walk around it several times, accompanied by myself.

—ERIC SATIE

Composing a piece of music is very feminine. It is sensitive, emotional, contemplative. By comparison, doing housework is positively masculine.

—BARBARA KOLB

I certainly had no feeling for harmony, and Schoenberg thought that that would make it impossible for me to write music. He said, 'You'll come to a wall you won't be able to get through.' So I said, 'I'll beat my head against that wall.'

—JOHN CAGE

If a composer could say what he had to say in words he would not bother trying to say it in music.

—GUSTAV MAHLER

In order to compose, all you need to do is remember a tune that nobody else has thought of.

—ROBERT SCHUMANN

A good composer does not imitate; he steals.

—IGOR STRAVINSKY

You can't stop. Composing's not voluntary, you know. There's no choice, you're not free. You're landed with an idea and you have responsibility to that idea.

—HARRISON BIRTWISTLE

Composing is like driving down a foggy road...

—BENJAMIN BRITTEN

When music fails to agree to the ear, to soothe the ear the heart and the senses, then it has missed the point.

—MARIA CALLAS

Anton Bruckner wrote the same symphony nine times, trying to get it just right. He failed.

—SIR THOMAS BEECHAM
on Bruckner's Seventh Symphony

That's the way Stravinsky was—bup, bup, bup— The poor guy's dead now. Play it legato.

—EUGENE ORMANDY

The melody is generally what the piece is all about.

—AARON COPLAND

If the reader were so rash as to purchase any of Bela Bartok's compositions, he would find that they each and all consist of unmeaning bunches of notes, apparently representing the composer promenading the keyboard in his boots. Some can be played better with the elbows, others with the flat of the hand. None require fingers to perform or ears to listen too.

—FREDERICK CORDER

After all, the central nervous system can accommodate only so many pages of persistent pianissimos, chord clusters in the marge, and tritons on the vibes. Sooner or later, the diet palls and the patient cries out for a cool draught of C major.

—GLENN GOULD

There are plenty of good pieces waiting to be written in C Major.

—ARNOLD SCHOENBERG

The public doesn't want new music; the main thing it demands of a composer is that he be dead.

—ARTHUR HONEGGER

BACH! A colossal syllable, one which makes composers tremble, brings performers to their knees, beatifies the Bach-lover, and apparently bores the daylights out of everyone else.

—LEONARD BERNSTEIN

Bach is Bach, as God is God.

—HECTOR BERLIOZ

If Bach is not in Heaven... I am not going!

—WILLIAM F. BUCKLEY, JR.

It is a sobering thought that when Mozart was my age he had already been dead for two years.

—Tom Lehrer

Mozart died too late rather than too soon.

—Glenn Gould

Mozart is happiness before it has gotten defined.

—Arthur Miller

I write [music] as a sow piddles.

—Wolfgang Amadeus Mozart

I occasionally play works by contemporary composers and for two reasons. First, to discourage the composer from writing any more, and secondly to remind myself how much I appreciate Beethoven.

—JASCHA HEIFETZ

What can you do with it? It's like a lot of yaks jumping about.

—SIR THOMAS BEECHAM
on Beethoven's Seventh Symphony

Rossini would have been a great composer if his teacher had spanked him enough on his backside.

—LUDWIG VAN BEETHOVEN

There are some experiences in life which should not be demanded twice from any man, and one of them is listening to the Brahms Requiem.

—George Bernard Shaw

Why waste money on psychotherapy when you can listen to the B Minor Mass?

—Michael Torke

Life can't be all bad when for ten dollars you can buy all the Beethoven sonatas and listen to them for ten years.

—William F. Buckley, Jr.

Wagner's music is better than it sounds.

—Mark Twain

I like Wagner's music better than any other music. It is so loud that one can talk the whole time without other people hearing what one says. That is a great advantage.

—OSCAR WILDE

You only have time to clamber up a tree and hold on like a grim death. Your hair is blown about, your face is streaked with blood, but when the storm dies off and recedes a little, you get down from your shelter, you shake yourself and you enjoy the pleasure of having escaped a great danger. The hurricane, my dear child, is Wagner or Wagnerism. It is fearsome, but it passes on. The important thing is not to let yourself be carried away.

—CHARLES GOUNOD

I love Wagner, but the music I prefer is that of a cat hung up by its tail outside a window and trying to stick to the panes of glass with its claws.

—CHARLES BAUDELAIRE

There are two means of refuge from the miseries of life: music and cats.

—ALBERT SCHWEITZER

I can't listen to that much Wagner. I start getting the urge to conquer Poland.

—WOODY ALLEN

Move your neck according to the music.

—ETHIOPIAN PROVERB

If you can walk you can dance. If you can talk you can sing.

—Zimbabwe proverb

Music melts all the separate parts of our bodies together.

—Anais Nin

Music is a beautiful opiate, if you don't take it too seriously.

—Henry Miller

Take a music bath once or twice a week for a few seasons, and you will find that it is to the soul what the water-bath is to the body.

—Oliver Wendell Holmes

Music washes away from the soul the dust of everyday life.

—Red Auerbach

Music is a higher revelation than all wisdom and philosophy. Music is the electrical soil in which the spirit lives, thinks and invents.

—Ludwig van Beethoven

Music has a power of forming the character, and should therefore be introduced into the education of the young.

—Aristotle

Music is the silence between the notes.

—Claude Debussy

After silence, that which comes nearest to express-
ing the inexpressible, is music.

—ALDOUS HUXLEY

Music is essentially useless, as life is.

—GEORGE SANTAYANA

[Music] can be made anywhere, is invisible and
does not smell.

—W. H. AUDEN.

Music can name the unnamable and communicate
the unknowable.

—LEONARD BERNSTEIN

Beautiful music is the art of the prophets that can calm the agitations of the soul; it is one of the most magnificent and delightful presents God has given us.

—MARTIN LUTHER

Information is not knowledge. Knowledge is not wisdom. Wisdom is not truth. Truth is not beauty. Beauty is not love. Love is not music. Music is best.

—FRANK ZAPPA

The odd thing about music is that we understand and respond to it without actually having to learn it. Each word in a verbal phrase tells something all by itself; it has a history and nuances. But musical tones mean something only in relation to one another, when they're teamed up. You needn't understand the tones to be moved.

—DIANE ACKERMAN

With music we are trapped in time. Each note is gone as soon as it has sounded and it never can be recontemplated or heard again at the particular instant of rightness. It is always too late for a second look.

—LEONARD BERNSTEIN

Since music is a language with some meaning at least for the immense majority of mankind, although only a tiny minority of people are capable of formulating a meaning in it, and since it is the only language with the contradictory attributes of being at once intelligible and untranslatable, the musical creator is a being comparable to the gods, and music itself the supreme mystery of the science of man, a mystery that all the various disciplines come up against and which holds the key to their progress.

—CLAUDE LÉVI-STRAUSS

Speech is man's most confused and egocentric expression, his most orderly and magnanimous utterance is music.

—NED ROREM

Let a man be stimulated by poetry, established by the rules of propriety, and perfected by music.

—CONFUCIUS

Music begins where words are powerless to express. Music is made for the inexpressible. I want music to seem to rise from the shadows and indeed sometimes to return to them.

—CLAUDE DEBUSSY

Music has its own alphabet of only seven letters, as compared with the twenty-six of the English alphabet. Each of these letters represents a note, and just as certain letters are complete words in themselves, so certain notes may stand alone, with the force of a whole word.

—SIGMUND SPAETH

Music, theoretically considered, consists altogether of lines of tone. It more nearly resembles a picture or an architectural drawing, than any other art creation; the difference being that in a drawing the lines are visible and constant, while in music they are audible and in motion. The separate tones are the points through which the lines are drawn; and the impression which is intended, and which is apprehended by the intelligent listener, is not that of single tones, but of continuous lines of tones, describing movements, curves and angles, rising, falling, poising—directly analogous to the linear impressions conveyed by a picture or drawing.

—PERCY GOETSCHIUS

There is geometry in the humming of the strings.
There is music in the spacing of the spheres.

—PYTHAGORAS

Music creates order out of chaos: for rhythm imposes
unanimity upon the divergent, melody imposes con-
tinuity upon the disjointed, and harmony imposes
compatibility upon the incongruous.

—YEHUDI MENUHIN

The integration of recent insights in physics and
the life sciences will require "a conceptual shift
from structure to rhythm." Theorists now describe
atoms in terms of harmonics; molecules vibrate;
each substance is "tuned" to a unique pitch; plants
and animals undergo cycles of growth and rest;
planets fall into resonant orbits; stars oscillate,
and galaxies whirl a majestic spiral dance.

—RICHARD HEINBERG

It occurred to me by intuition, and music was the driving force behind that intuition. My discovery was the result of musical perception.

—ALBERT EINSTEIN,
when asked about his theory of relativity

The rotation of the universe and the motion of the planets could neither begin nor continue without music... for everything is ordered by God according to the laws of harmony.

—PLUTARCH

Music is the pleasure the human mind experiences from counting without being aware that it is counting.

—GOTTFRIED LEIBNIZ

It is proportion that beautifies everything, the whole universe consists of it, and music is measured by it.

—ORLANDO GIBBONS

Mathematicians are able to break down into measure and figure what musicians do intuitively. The art of music is endowed with a supernatural origin and a divine purpose, more so than any other art.

—GOTTFRIED LIEBNIZ

Music is a moral law. It gives a soul to the universe, wings to the mind, flight to the imagination, a charm to sadness and life to everything. Fine music is the essence of order and leads to all that is just and good, of which it is the invisible, but nevertheless dazzling, passionate and eternal form.

—PLATO

The power of music to integrate and cure...is quite fundamental. [It is the] profoundest non-chemical medication.

—OLIVER SACKS

Instead of using what we can guess at about the nature of thought to explain the nature of music start over again. Begin with music and see what it can tell us about the sensation of thinking. Music is the effort we make to explain to ourselves how our brains work.... If you want...to hear the whole mind working, all at once, put on the *St. Matthew Passion* and turn the volume up all the way. That is the sound of the whole central nervous system of human beings, all at once.

—LEWIS THOMAS

[Rhythm] is there in the cycles of the seasons, in the migrations of the birds and animals, in the fruiting and withering of plants, and in the birth, maturation and death of ourselves.

—MICKEY HART

All the sounds of the earth are like music.

—OSCAR HAMMERSTEIN

Mockingbirds don't do one thing but make music for us to enjoy. They don't eat up people's gardens, don't nest in corncribs, they don't do one thing but sing their hearts out for us. That's why it's a sin to kill a mockingbird.

—HARPER LEE

Enough of clouds, waves, aquariums, water-sprites and nocturnal scents; what we need is a music of the earth, everyday music...music one can live in like a house.

—Jean Cocteau

Musick is a tonick to the saddened soul, a Roaring Meg against Melancholy, to rear and revive the languishing soul, affecting not only the ears, but the very arteries, the vital and animal spirits; it erects the mind, and makes it nimble.

—Robert Burton

Music begins to atrophy when it departs too far from the dance...poetry begins to atrophy when it gets too far from music; but this must not be taken as implying that all good music is dance music or all poetry lyric. Bach and Mozart are never too far from physical movement.

—Ezra Pound

Truly fertile Music, the only kind that will move us, that we shall truly appreciate, will be a Music conducive to Dream, which banishes all reason and analysis.

—ALBERT CAMUS

What is best in music is not to be found in the notes.

—GUSTAV MAHLER

My heart, which is so full to overflowing,
has often been solaced and refreshed
by music, when sick and weary.

—MARTIN LUTHER KING, JR.

Life is a score that we play at sight, not merely before we have divined the intentions of the composer, but even before we have mastered our instruments; even worse, a large part of the score has been only roughly indicated, and we must improvise the music for our particular instrument, over long passages. On these terms, the whole operation seems one of endless difficulty and frustration; and indeed, were it not for the fact that some of the passages have been played so often by our predecessors that, when we come to them, we seem to recall some of the score and can anticipate the natural sequence of the notes, we might often give up in sheer despair. The wonder is not that so much cacophony appears in our actual individual lives, but that there is any appearance of harmony and progression.

—LEWIS MUMFORD

Les plus desesperes sont les chants les plus beaux.
(The most beautiful songs are the saddest songs.)

—ALFRED DE MUSSET

It requires wisdom to understand wisdom: the music is nothing if the audience is deaf.

—WALTER LIPPMAN

A painter paints his pictures on canvas. But musicians paint their pictures on silence. We provide the music, and you provide the silence.

—LEOPOLD STOKOWSKI,
reprimanding a talkative audience

Applause is a receipt, not a bill.

—ARTUR SCHNABEL

Musical people are so absurdly unreasonable. They always want one to be perfectly dumb at the very moment when one is longing to be absolutely deaf.

—OSCAR WILDE

I've never known a musician who regretted being one. Whatever deceptions life may have in store for you, music itself is not going to let you down.

—VIRGIL THOMSON

It is better to make a piece of music than to perform one, better to perform one than to listen to one, better to listen to one than to misuse it as a means of distraction, entertainment, or acquisition of 'culture'.

—JOHN CAGE

Where words fail, music speaks.

—HANS CHRISTIAN ANDERSEN

It was music of kind I had never heard before. It was music that demanded physical response, patting of the feet, drumming of the fingers, or nodding of the head in time with the beat. The barbaric harmonies, the audacious resolutions...the intricate rhythms... produced a most curious effect.

—JAMES WELDON JOHNSON, on hearing ragtime music

I've come close to matching the feeling of that night in 1944 in music, when I first heard Diz and Bird, but I've never got there.... I'm always looking for it, listening and feeling for it, though, trying to always feel it in and through the music I play every day.

—MILES DAVIS

Jazz is my adventure.

—THELONIUS MONK

Jazz music is an intensified feeling of nonchalance.

—FRANÇOISE SAGAN

Blues is a good woman feeling bad.

—THOMAS DORSEY

Sounds like the blues are composed of feeling, finesse, and fear.

—BILLY GIBBONS

A jazz musician is a juggler who uses harmonies instead of oranges.

—BENNY GREEN

Playing 'bop' is like playing scrabble with all the vowels missing.

—Duke Ellington

You can't play the blues in an air-conditioned room.

—Matt "Guitar" Murphy

What 'jazz' means to me is the worst kind of working conditions, the worst in cultural prejudice... The term 'jazz' has come to mean the abuse and exploitation of black musicians.

—Max Roach

Jazz is the art form of the outsider, whether racially, musically, or psychologically.

—Ted Gioia

Music to me is like breathing—I don't get tired of breathing, I don't get tired of music.

—RAY CHARLES

Bach gave us God's Word. Mozart gave us God's laughter. Beethoven gave us God's fire. God gave us Music that we might pray without words.

—QUOTE FROM OUTSIDE AN OLD OPERA HOUSE

Bach almost persuades me to be a Christian.

—ROGER FRY

Schnabel's performances in the last years were like looking at the sun without dark glasses.

—EDWARD CRANKSHAW

Since I am coming to that holy room,
Where, with thy choir of saints for evermore
I shall be made thy music; as I come
I tune the instrument here at the door,
And what I must do then, think now before.

—JOHN DONNE

Always give them the old fire, even when you feel
like a squashed cake of ice.

—ETHEL MERMAN

Modern music is as dangerous as narcotics.

—PIETRO MASCAGNI

In music the passions enjoy themselves.

—FRIEDRICH NIETZSCHE

All passionate language does of itself become musical.... The speech of a man even in zealous anger becomes a chant, a song.

—THOMAS CARLYLE

In sweet music is such art,
Killing care and grief of heart
Fall asleep, or hearing die.

—WILLIAM SHAKESPEARE

Music hath charms to soothe a savage breast
To soften rocks, or bend a knotted oak.

—WILLIAM CONGREVE

Music is spiritual. The music business is not.

—VAN MORRISON

The music business is a cruel and shallow trench, a long plastic hallway where thieves and pimps run free, and good men lie like dogs. There is also a negative side.

—Hunter S. Thomson

Music is everybody's possession. It's only publishers who think that people own it.

—John Lennon

Making music should not be left to the professionals.

—Michelle Shocked

Hell is full of musical amateurs: music is the brandy of the damned.

—George Bernard Shaw

I don't know anything about music. In my line you don't have to.

—ELVIS PRESLEY

I don't believe in having bands for solo records.

—MICK JAGGER

I hate music, especially when it's played.

—JIMMY DURANTE

I don't listen to music. I hate all music.

—JOHNNY ROTTEN

Which is more musical: a truck passing by a factory or a truck passing by a music school?

—JOHN CAGE

Too many pieces of music finish too long after the end.

—Igor Stravinsky

It's just a song man; it doesn't mean anything.

—John Lennon

Rock 'n Roll is monotony tinged with hysteria.

—Vance Packard

Music is a safe kind of high.

—Jimi Hendrix

I've always felt rock and roll was very, very wholesome music.

—Aretha Franklin

Rock music should be gross: that's the fun of it. It gets up and drops its trousers.

—Bruce Dickinson

Rock and roll is the hamburger that ate the world.

—Peter York

At it's best, punk music represents a fundamental and age-old Utopian dream: that if you give people the license to be as outrageous as they want in absolutely any fashion they can dream up, they'll be creative about it, and do something good besides.

—Lester Bangs

New music? Hell, there's been no new music since Stravinsky.

—Duke Ellington

My music is best understood by children and animals.

—IGOR STRAVINSKY

Poetry and Hums aren't things which you get, they're things which get you. And all you can do is to go where they can find you.

—A. A. MILNE, spoken by Winnie the Pooh

It is the stretched soul that makes music, and souls are stretched by the pull of opposites—opposite bents, tastes, yearnings, loyalties. Where there is no polarity—where energies flow smoothly in one direction—there will be much doing but no music.

—ERIC HOFFER

Every work of art has two faces, one directed towards eternity and the other towards its own time. The part that remains is the spirit of the work, its essence. A musical composition should be seen as existing by itself and for itself, and not as having been created for a purpose, however positive or beneficial. As human beings we do not possess infinite qualities, but as musicians I believe we can extend our finite power to a point where we can create an illusion of infinity. It is only by knowing ourselves that we come to know the things outside ourselves.

—Daniel Barenboim

You may be sitting in a room reading this book. Imagine one note struck upon the piano. Immediately that one note is enough to change the atmosphere of the room—proving that the sound element in music is a powerful and mysterious agent, which it would be foolish to deride or belittle.

—Aaron Copland

There is sweet music here that softer falls
Than petals from blown roses on the grass,
Or night dews on still waters between walls
Of shadowy granite, in a gleaming pass;
Music that gentlier on the spirit lies
Than tired eyelids upon tired eyes.

—ALFRED, LORD TENNYSON

I haven't understood a bar of music in my life, but
I've felt it.

—IGOR STRAVINSKY

I have done what I could, and so, judge, my God.

—GABRIEL FAURE

Music makes one feel so romantic—at least it always
gets on one's nerves—which is the same thing
nowadays.

—OSCAR WILDE

Extraordinary how potent cheap music is.

—Noel Coward

Cocktail music is accepted as audible wallpaper.

—Alistair Cooke.

Music with dinner is an insult both to the cook and the violinist.

—G. K. Chesterton

I know canned music makes chickens lay more eggs and factory workers produce more. But how much more can they get out of you on an elevator?

—Victor Borge

Whatever else it may be—stimulus, tranquilizer, aural nipple, too of executives, Muzak is basically trivializing. It is not simply that it relegates music to the province of wallpaper. Background music never need be banal. When it is used in support of drama, it can greatly enhance without harming itself.... In such uses, music collaborates with artists, it becomes an art among arts. But Muzak collaborates chiefly with management: it is used as an aural smoke-screen, a form of jamming, a hormone in the henhouse, an emollient in cemeteries.

—NORMAN CORWIN

People whose sensibility is destroyed by music in trains, airports, lifts, cannot concentrate on a Beethoven Quartet.

—WITOLD LUTOSLAWSKI

Brass bands are all very well in their place—out-doors and several miles away.

—Sir Thomas Beecham

Military justice is to justice what military music is to music.

—Groucho Marx

If you can imagine a man having a vasectomy without anesthetic to the sound of frantic sitar-playing, you will have some idea what popular Turkish music is like.

—Bill Bryson

The piano is a monster that screams when you touch its teeth.

—Andre Segovia, guitarist

Two skeletons copulating on a corrugated tin roof.

—SIR THOMAS BEECHAM, describing the harpsichord

Harpists spend ninety percent of their lives tuning their harps and ten percent playing out of tune.

—IGOR STRAVINSKY

An oboe is an ill-wind that nobody blows good.

—BENNET CERF

I got to try the bagpipes. It was like trying to blow an octopus.

—JAMES GALWAY

There are two instruments worse than a clarinet—two clarinets.

—AMBROSE BIERCE

Nothing is more beautiful than a guitar, except, possibly, two.

—Frederic Chopin

Is it not strange that sheep's guts should hale souls out of men's bodies?

—William Shakespeare

Precisely because we do not communicate by singing, a song can be out of place but not out of character; its is just as credible that a stupid person should sing beautifully as that a clever person should do so.

—W. H. Auden

Ride a cock-horse to Banbury-Cross,
To see an old woman get up on her horse.
Rings on her fingers, and bells on her toes,
And so she makes music wherever she goes.

—MOTHER GOOSE

As an art grows more and more complex and dense, the number of relations among simple elements increases until those relations look like extraordinarily refined experiences denied to the common herd.... Yet there is no real barrier to be leaped over by an effort of genius between understanding a "vulgar" dance tune and a Beethoven symphony.

—JACQUES BARZUN

The basic difference between classical music and jazz is that in the former the music is always greater than its performance—Beethoven's Violin Concerto, for instance, is always greater than its performance—whereas the way jazz is performed is always more important than what is being performed.

—ANDRÉ PREVIN

I believe that interpretation should be like a transparent glass, a window for the composer's music.

—VLADIMIR ASHKENAZY

Music, as long as it exists, will always take its departure from the major triad and return to it. The musician cannot escape it any more than the painter his primary colors or the architect his three dimensions.

—PAUL HINDEMITH

Music resembles poetry; in each are nameless graces which no methods teach, And which a master-hand alone can reach.

—ALEXANDER POPE

A poet always has too many words in his vocabulary, a painter too many colors on his palette, a musician too many notes on his keyboard.

—JEAN COCTEAU

The trouble with music appreciation in general is that people are taught to have too much respect for music; they should be taught to love it instead.

—IGOR STRAVINSKY

Learning music by reading about it is like making love by mail.

—ISSAC STERN

Writing about music is like dancing about architecture—it's really a stupid thing to want to do.

—ELVIS COSTELLO

A musicologist is a man who can read music but cannot hear it.

—SIR THOMAS BEECHAM

We cannot describe sound, but we cannot forget it either.

—IGOR STRAVINSKY

Who can deny that the Queensborough Bridge is the work of a creative artist? It never fails to give me a poignant desire to capture the noble cadence of its music.

—HELEN KELLER

Architecture is frozen music.

—JOHANN WOLFGANG VON GOETHE

There's a barrel-organ carolling across a golden
    street,
In the city as the sun sinks low;
And the music's not immortal; but the world
    has made it sweet
And fulfilled it with the sunset glow.

—ALFRED NOYES

Fortissimo at last!

—GUSTAV MAHLER, on seeing Niagara Falls

Something about the idea of breath or wind entering a piece of wood and filling it roundly with a vital cry—a sound—has captivated us for millennia. It's like the spirit of life playing through the whole length of a person's body. It's as if we could breath into the trees and make them speak. We hold a branch in our hands, blow into it, and it groans, it sings.

—DIANE ACKERMAN

Music, of all the arts, stands in a special region, unlit by any star but its own, and utterly without meaning...except its own.

—LEONARD BERNSTEIN.

Music means nothing but itself.

—STRAVINSKY

The trouble with real life is that there's no danger music.

—Lou Holtz, Jr.
(spoken by Jim Carrey in *The Cable Guy*)